GREEN DAY.

PRESENTS

american idiot

Special thanks to Rob Cavallo

Project Managers: Jeannette DeLisa and Aaron Stang
Album Art: © 2004 Reprise Records
Art Direction and Design: Chris Bilheimer
Book Art Layout: Joe Klucar

CONTENTS

ⒶMERICAN IDIOT *FEB 23*

1. DON'T WANT TO BE AN AMERICAN IDIOT
   DON'T WANT A NATION UNDER THE NEW MANIA
   CAN YOU HEAR THE SOUND OF HYSTERIA?
   THE SUBLIMINAL MIND FUCK AMERICA
   WELCOME TO A NEW KIND OF TENSION
   ALL ACROSS THE ALIENATION
   WHERE EVERYTHING ISN'T MEANT TO BE O.K.
   TELEVISION DREAMS OF TOMORROW
   → WE'RE NOT THE ONES MEANT TO FOLLOW
   FOR THAT'S ENOUGH TO ARGUE
   MAYBE I AM THE FAGGOT AMERICA
   I'M NOT A PART OF A REDNECK AGENDA
   → NOW EVERYBODY DO THE PROPAGANDA!
   AND SING ALONG TO THE AGE OF PARANOIA
   DON'T WANT TO BE AN AMERICAN IDIOT
   ONE NATION ~~CONTROLLED BY~~ THE ~~NEW~~ MEDIA
   → INFORMATION AGE OF HYSTERIA
   CALLING OUT TO IDIOT AMERICA™

2. JESUS OF SUBURBIA *MAR.3   JINGLETOWN USA*

   I.   I'M THE SON OF RAGE AND LOVE
        THE JESUS OF SUBURBIA
        FROM THE BIBLE OF "NONE OF THE ABOVE"
        ON A STEADY DIET OF SODA POP AND RITALIN
        NO ONE EVER DIED FOR MY SINS IN HELL
        AS FAR AS I CAN TELL ⟶

AT LEAST THE ONES I GOT AWAY WITH
BUT THERE'S NOTHING WRONG WITH ME
THIS IS HOW I'M SUPPOSED TO BE
→ IN THE LAND OF MAKE BELIEVE
THAT DON'T BELIEVE IN ME
GET MY TELEVISION FIX SITTING ON MY CRUCIFIX
THE LIVING ROOM IN MY PRIVATE WOMB
WHILE THE MOM'S & BRAD'S ARE AWAY
TO FALL IN LOVE AND FALL IN DEBT
TO ALCOHOL AND CIGARETTES AND MARY JANE
TO KEEP ME INSANE AND DOING SOMEONE ELSE'S COCAINE

II. CITY OF THE DAMNED
AT THE CENTER OF THE EARTH
IN THE PARKING LOT OF THE 7-11 WHERE I WAS TAUGHT
THE MOTTO WAS JUST A LIE
IT SAYS "HOME IS WHERE YOUR HEART IS"
BUT WHAT A SHAME
'CAUSE EVERYONE'S HEART DOESN'T BEAT THE SAME
WE'RE BEATING OUT OF TIME
CITY OF THE DEAD
AT THE END OF ANOTHER LOST HIGHWAY
SIGNS MISLEADING TO NOWHERE - CITY OF THE DAMNED
LOST CHILDREN WITH DIRTY FACES TODAY
NO ONE REALLY SEEMS TO CARE
I READ THE GRAFFITI ~~IN THE TOILET~~ IN THE BATHROOM STALL
LIKE THE HOLY SCRIPTURES IN A SHOPPING MALL
AND SO IT SEEMED TO CONFESS IT DIDN'T SAY MUCH

BUT IT ONLY CONFIRMED THAT.
THE **CENTER OF THE EARTH** IS **THE END OF THE WORLD**
AND I COULD REALLY CARE LESS

III. [I DON'T CARE] I DON'T CARE IF YOU DON'T. I DON'T CARE IF YOU DON'T. I DON'T CARE IF YOU DON'T CARE. EVERYONE IS SO FULL OF SHIT! BORN AND RAISED BY HYPOCRITES. HEARTS RECYCLED BUT NEVER SAVED. FROM THE CRADLE TO THE GRAVE. WE ARE THE KIDS OF WAR AND PEACE. FROM ANAHEIM TO THE MIDDLE EAST. WE ARE THE STORIES AND DISCIPLES OF THE JESUS OF SUBURBIA, LAND OF MAKE BELIEVE AND IT DON'T BELIEVE IN ME AND I DON'T CARE!

IV. Dearly Beloved
DEARLY BELOVED, ARE YOU LISTENING?
I CAN'T REMEMBER A WORD THAT YOU WERE SAYING
      ARE WE DEMENTED?
      OR AM I DISTURBED?
THE SPACE THAT'S INBETWEEN INSANE AND INSECURE
OH THERAPY, CAN YOU PLEASE FILL THE VOID?
      AM I RETARDED?
      OR AM I JUST OVERJOYED?
NOBODY'S PERFECT AND I STAND ACCUSED
FOR LACK OF A BETTER WORD AND THAT'S MY BEST EXCUSE

V. TALES OF ANOTHER BROKEN HOME
TO LIVE AND NOT TO BREATHE
IS TO DIE IN TRAGEDY
TO RUN, TO RUN AWAY TO FIND WHAT TO BELIEVE
AND I LEAVE BEHIND THIS HURRICANE OF FUCKING LIES
I LOST MY FAITH TO THIS, THIS TOWN THAT DON'T EXIST
SO I RUN, I RUN AWAY
TO THE LIGHT OF MASOCHISTS
AND I LEAVE BEHIND THIS HURRICANE OF FUCKING LIES
AND I WALKED THIS LINE A MILLION AND ONE FUCKING TIMES
BUT NOT THIS TIME
i don't feel any shame, i won't apologize
WHEN THERE AIN'T NOWHERE YOU CAN GO
RUNNING AWAY FROM PAIN WHEN YOU'VE BEEN VICTIMIZED

TALES FROM ANOTHER BROKEN HOME

#3. HOLIDAY — APRIL 1st IN THE CITY

#3. HEAR THE SOUND OF THE FALLING RAIN,
COMING DOWN LIKE AN ARMAGEDDON FLAME
THE SHAME
THE ONES WHO DIED WITHOUT A NAME
HEAR THE DOGS HOWLING OUT OF KEY
TO A HYMN CALLED "FAITH AND MISERY"
AND BLEED THE COMPANY LOST THE WAR TODAY

★ I BEG TO DREAM AND DIFFER FROM THE HOLLOW LIES
THIS IS THE DAWNING OF THE REST OF OUR LIVES
ON HOLIDAY
HEAR THE DRUM POUNDING OUT OF TIME
ANOTHER PROTESTER HAS CROSSED THE LINE
TO FIND THE MONEY'S ON THE OTHER SIDE
CAN I GET ANOTHER **AMEN**?
THERE'S A **FLAG** WRAPPED AROUND A SCORE OF MEN
A GAG
A **PLASTIC BAG** ON A MONUMENT
✝ THE REPRESENTATIVE OF CALIFORNIA HAS THE FLOOR
ZIEG HEIL TO THE PRESIDENT GASMAN
BOMBS AWAY IS YOUR PUNISHMENT
PULVERIZE THE EIFFEL TOWERS
WHO CRITICIZE YOUR GOVERNMENT
BANG **BANG** GOES THE BROKEN GLASS
KILL ALL THE FAGS THAT DON'T AGREE
TRIALS BY FIRE SETTING FIRE
IS NOT A WAY THAT'S MEANT FOR ME

JUSTCAUSE — JUSTCAUSE BECAUSE WE'RE OUTLAWS YEAH!
I BEG TO DREAM AND DIFFER FROM THE HOLLOW LIES
THIS IS THE DAWNING OF THE REST OF OUR LIVES
THIS IS OUR LIVES ON HOLIDAY

4. BOULEVARD OF BROKEN DREAMS BLVD

APRIL 2 I WALK A LONELY ROAD
THE ONLY ONE THAT I HAVE EVER KNOWN
DON'T KNOW WHERE IT GOES
BUT IT'S HOME TO ME AND I WALK ALONE
I WALK THIS EMPTY STREET
ON THE BLVD. OF BROKEN DREAMS
WHERE THE CITY SLEEPS
AND I'M THE ONLY ONE AND I WALK ALONE
I WALK ALONE. I WALK ALONE. I WALK ALONE. I WALK ALONE.
MY SHADOW'S THE ONLY ONE THAT WALKS BESIDE ME
MY SHALLOW HEART'S THE ONLY THING THAT'S BEATING
SOMETIMES I WISH SOMEONE OUT THERE WILL FIND ME
'TIL THEN I WALK ALONE
I'M WALKING DOWN THE LINE
THAT DIVIDES ME SOMEWHERE IN MY MIND
ON THE BORDERLINE OF THE EDGE
AND WHERE I WALK ALONE
READ BETWEEN THE LINES OF WHAT'S
FUCKED UP AND EVERYTHING'S ALRIGHT
CHECK MY VITAL SIGNS TO KNOW I'M STILL ALIVE

AND I WALK ALONE
I WALK ALONE, I WALK ALONE. I WALK ALONE. I WALK ALONE
I WALK THIS EMPTY STREET ON THE BLVD. OF BROKEN DREAMS
WHERE THE CITY SLEEPS [redacted]
AND I'M THE ONLY ONE AND I WALK ALONE
MY SHADOW'S THE ONLY ONE THAT WALKS BESIDE ME
MY SHALLOW HEART'S THE ONLY THING THAT'S BEATING
SOMETIMES I WISH SOMEONE OUT THERE WILL FIND ME
'TIL THEN, I WALK ALONE

5. Are We The Waiting

EASTER SUNDAY

ARE WE WE ARE ~~THE~~ ARE WE WE ARE THE WAITING UNKNOWN

STARRY NIGHTS CITY LIGHTS
COMING DOWN OVER ME
SKY SCRAPERS AND STARGAZERS IN MY HEAD
ARE WE WE ARE, ARE WE [redacted] WE ARE THE WAITING UNKNOWN
THIS DIRTY TOWN WAS BURNING DOWN IN MY DREAMS
LOST AND FOUND CITY BOUND IN MY DREAMS & SCREAMING
ARE WE WE ARE, ARE WE WE ARE THE WAITING AND
SCREAMING ARE WE WE ARE ARE WE WE ARE THE WAITING
FORGET ME NOTS AND SECOND THOUGHTS
LIVE IN ISOLATION
HEADS OR TAILS AND FAIRYTALES IN MY MIND
ARE WE WE ARE, ARE WE WE ARE THE WAITING UNKNOWN
THE **RAGE AND LOVE**, THE STORY OF MY LIFE
THE **JESUS OF SUBURBIA** IS A LIE & SCREAMING
ARE WE WE ARE, ARE WE WE ARE THE WAITING UNKNOWN
ARE WE WE ARE, ARE WE WE [redacted] ARE THE WAITING UNKNOWN
ARE WE WE ARE, ARE WE WE ARE THE WAITING UNKNOWN
ARE WE WE ARE, ARE WE WE ARE THE WAITING UNKNOWN

6. St. Jimmy

MAY 7

ST. JIMMY'S COMING DOWN ACROSS THE ALLEYWAY
UPON THE BLVD. LIKE A ZIP GUN ON PARADE
LIGHT OF A SILHOUETTE, HE'S INSUBORDINATE
COMING AT YOU ON THE COUNT OF 1, 2, 3, 4
MY NAME IS JIMMY AND YOU BETTER NOT WEAR IT OUT.
SUICIDE COMMANDO THAT YOUR MOMMA TALKED ABOUT. KING
OF THE 40 THIEVES AND I'M HERE TO [redacted] REPRESENT THE
NEEDLE IN THE VEIN OF THE ESTABLISHMENT. I'M THE
PATRON SAINT OF THE DENIAL WITH AN **ANGEL FACE** AND
A TASTE FOR SUICIDAL CIGARETTES AND RAMEN AND A
LITTLE BAG OF DOPE. I AM THE SON OF A BITCH AND EDGAR
ALLAN POE, RAISED IN THE CITY UNDER A HALO OF LIGHTS.
THE PRODUCT OF WAR AND FEAR THAT WE'VE BEEN VICTIMIZED.
ARE YOU TALKING TO ME? MY NAME IS ST. JIMMY. I'M A
SON OF A GUN. I'M THE ONE THAT'S FROM THE WAY OUTSIDE.
I'M A TEENAGE ASSASSIN EXECUTING SOME FUN IN THE CULT
OF THE LIFE OF CRIME. I'D REALLY HATE TO SAY IT, BUT I
TOLD YOU SO. SO SHUT YOUR [redacted] MOUTH BEFORE I SHOOT YOU DOWN
[redacted] OL' BOY. WELCOME TO THE CLUB AND GIVE ME SOME BLOOD.
I'M THE RESIDENT LEADER OF THE LOST AND FOUND. IT'S COMEDY
AND TRAGEDY. IT'S ST. JIMMY, AND THAT'S MY NAME
AND DON'T WEAR IT OUT

7. GIVE ME NOVACAINE

JUNE 13

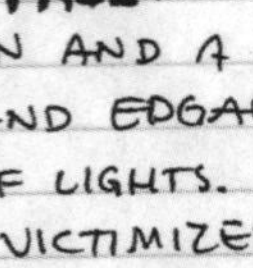

TAKE AWAY THE SENSATION INSIDE
BITTERSWEET MIGRAINE IN MY HEAD

IT'S LIKE A THROBBING TOOTHACHE OF THE MIND
I CAN'T TAKE THIS FEELING ANY MORE
DRAIN THE PRESSURE FROM THE SWELLING
THIS SENSATION'S OVER WHELMING
GIVE ME A LONG KISS GOODNIGHT
AND EVERYTHING WILL BE ALRIGHT
TELL ME THAT I WON'T FEEL A THING
GIVE ME NOVACAINE
OUT OF BODY AND OUT OF MIND
KISS THE DEMONS OUT OF MY DREAMS
I GET THE FUNNY FEELING AND THAT'S ALRIGHT
JIMMY SAYS IT'S BETTER THAN HERE
DRAIN THE PRESSURE FROM THE SWELLING
THIS SENSATION'S OVER WHELMING
GIVE ME A LONG KISS GOOD NIGHT
AND EVERYTHING WILL BE ALRIGHT
TELL ME JIMMY I WON'T FEEL A THING

GIVE ME NOVA CAINE

SHE'S A REBEL		8		JULY 4
	SHE'S A REBEL		FROM CHICAGO	
	SHE'S A SAINT		TO TORONTO	
	SHE'S THE SALT OF THE EARTH		SHE'S THE ONE THAT THEY	
	AND SHE'S DANGEROUS		CALL OLD WHATSERNAME	
	SHE'S A REBEL		SHE'S THE SYMBOL	
	VIGILANTE		OF RESISTANCE	
	MISSING LINK ON THE BRINK		AND SHE'S HOLDING ON MY	
	OF DESTRUCTION		HEART LIKE A HANDGRENADE	

IS SHE THINKING	TWIST OF FATE
WHAT I'M THINKING?	OR A MELODY THAT
IS SHE THE MOTHER OF ALL BOMBS?	SHE SINGS THE REVOLUTION
GONNA DETONATE	THE DAWNING OF OUR LIVES
IS SHE TROUBLE	SHE BRINGS THIS LIBERATION
LIKE I'M TROUBLE?	THAT I JUST CAN'T DEFINE
MAKE IT A DOUBLE	NOTHING COMES TO MIND

SHE'S AN **EXTRAORDINARY GIRL** 9
IN AN ORDINARY WORLD
AND SHE CAN'T SEEM TO GET AWAY
he lacks the courage in his mind
like a child left behind
like a pet left in the rain
SHE'S ALL ALONE AGAIN
WIPING THE TEARS FROM HER EYES
some days he feels like dying
SHE GETS SO SICK OF CRYING
SHE SEES THE MIRROR OF HERSELF
AN IMAGE SHE WANTS TO SELL
TO ANYONE WILLING TO BUY
he steals the image in her kiss
from her heart's apocalypse
from the one called whatsername

SHE'S ALL ALONE AGAIN
WIPING THE TEARS FROM HER EYES
some days he feels like dying
some days it's not worth trying
now that they both are finding
SHE GETS SO SICK OF CRYING

Dear J,   AUG.18TH

LETTER BOMB

Where have all the bastards gone? The
underbelly stacks up ten high. The
dummy failed the crash test, now
collecting unemployment checks like
a flunkie along for the ride.
Where have all the riots gone as the
city's motto gets pulverized?
"What's in love is now in debt" on your birth certificate
So strike the fucking match to light this
fuse! The town bishop is an extortionist
and he don't even know that you exist.
Standing still when it's do or die, you
better run for your fucking life. It's not over
till you're underground. It's not over before
it's too late. This city's burning "It's not my burden".
It's not over before it's too late, there is nothing left
to analyze. Where will all the martyrs go when
the virus cures itself? And where will we all go
when it's too late?
You're not the Jesus of Suburbia
The St. Jimmy is a figment of your father's
rage and your mother's love.   -W

MADE ME THE IDIOT AMERICA. IT'S NOT OVER 'TIL YOU'RE
UNDERGROUND. IT'S NOT OVER BEFORE IT'S TOO LATE. THIS
CITY'S BURNING. "IT'S NOT MY BURDEN". IT'S NOT OVER BEFORE
IT'S TOO LATE. SHE SAID "I CAN'T TAKE THIS PLACE", I'M
LEAVING IT BEHIND. SHE SAID "I CAN'T TAKE THIS TOWN,
I'M LEAVING YOU TONIGHT"

SEPT.10 (WAKE ME UP WHEN SEPTEMBER ENDS)

11. SUMMER HAS COME AND PASSED
     THE INNOCENT CAN NEVER LAST
     WAKE ME UP WHEN SEPTEMBER ENDS
     LIKE MY FATHER'S COME TO PASS
     SEVEN YEARS HAS GONE SO FAST
     WAKE ME UP WHEN SEPTEMBER ENDS
     HERE COMES THE RAIN AGAIN
     FALLING FROM THE STARS
     DRENCHED IN MY PAIN AGAIN
     BECOMING WHO WE ARE
     AS MY MEMORY RESTS
     BUT NEVER FORGETS WHAT I LOST
     WAKE ME UP WHEN SEPTEMBER ENDS
     SUMMER HAS COME AND PASSED
     THE INNOCENT CAN NEVER LAST
     WAKE ME UP WHEN SEPTEMBER ENDS
     RING OUT THE BELLS AGAIN
     LIKE WE DID WHEN SPRING BEGAN
     WAKE ME UP WHEN SEPTEMBER ENDS
     HERE COMES THE RAIN AGAIN
     FALLING FROM THE STARS
     DRENCHED IN MY PAIN AGAIN
     BECOMING WHO WE ARE
     AS MY MEMORY RESTS
     BUT NEVER FORGETS WHAT I LOST
     WAKE ME UP WHEN SEPTEMBER ENDS

SUMMER HAS COME AND PASSED, THE INNOCENT CAN NEVER LAST
LIKE MY FATHER'S COME TO PASS, TWENTY YEARS HAS GONE SO FAST
WAKE ME UP WHEN SEPTEMBER ENDS

WAKE ME UP WHEN SEPTEMBER ENDS

12 HOMECOMING

I. THE DEATH OF ST. JIMMY OCT. 19

MY HEART IS BEATING FROM ME
I AM STANDING ALL ALONE. PLEASE CALL ME
ONLY IF YOU ARE COMING HOME
WASTE ANOTHER YEAR FLIES BY WASTE A NIGHT OR TWO
YOU TAUGHT ME HOW TO LIVE IN THE STREETS OF SHAME
WHERE YOU'VE LOST YOUR DREAMS IN THE RAIN
THERE'S NO SIGN OF HOPE
THE STEMS AND SEEDS OF THE LAST OF THE DOPE
THERE'S A GLOW OF LIGHT. THE ST. JIMMY IS THE SPARK IN THE NIGHT
BEARING GIFTS AND TRUST. THE FIXTURE IN THE CITY OF LUST.
"WHAT THE HELL'S YOUR NAME?"
WHAT'S YOUR PLEASURE AND WHAT'S YOUR PAIN?
DO YOU DREAM TOO MUCH?
DO YOU THINK WHAT YOU NEED IS A CRUTCH?
IN THE CROWD OF PAIN, ST. JIMMY COMES WITHOUT ANY SHAME
HE SAYS "WE'RE FUCKED UP"
BUT WE'RE NOT THE SAME
AND MOM AND DAD ARE THE ONES YOU CAN BLAME

JIMMY DIED TODAY.

HE BLEW HIS BRAINS OUT INTO THE BAY
IN THE STATE OF MIND
IN MY OWN PRIVATE SUICIDE

II. EAST 12TH ST.   AND NOBODY CARES AND NOBODY CARES

DOES ANYONE CARE IF NOBODY CARES?
AND NOBODY CARES AND NOBODY CARES
DOES ANYONE CARE IF NOBODY CARES?
JESUS FILLING OUT PAPERWORK NOW
AT THE FACILITY ON EAST 12TH ST
HE'S NOT LISTENING TO A WORD NOW
HE'S IN HIS OWN WORLD AND HE'S DAYDREAMING
HE'D RATHER BE DOING SOMETHING ELSE NOW
LIKE CIGARETTES AND COFFEE WITH THE UNDERBELLY
HIS LIFE ON THE LINE WITH ANXIETY NOW
AND SHE HAD ENOUGH
AND HE'S HAD PLENTY
SOMEBODY GET ME OUT OF HERE
ANYBODY GET ME OUT OF HERE
SOMEBODY GET ME OUT OF HERE
GET ME THE FUCK RIGHT OUT OF HERE
SO FAR AWAY, I DON'T WANT TO STAY
GET ME OUTTA HERE RIGHT NOW
I JUST WANT TO BE FREE
IS THERE A POSSIBILITY?
GET ME OUT OF HERE RIGHT NOW
THIS LIFELIKE DREAM AINT FOR ME

III. NOBODY LIKES YOU! NOV 10

I FELL ASLEEP WHILE WATCHING SPIKE TV AFTER 10 CUP'S OF COFFEE AND YOU'RE STILL NOT HERE. DREAMING OF A SONG WHEN SOMETHING WENT WRONG, BUT I CAN'T TELL ANYONE 'CUZ YOU'RE NOT HERE. LEFT ME HERE ALONE WHEN I SHOULD HAVE STAYED HOME AFTER 10 CUPS OF COFFEE I'M THINKING. WHERE'D YOU GO? NOBODY LIKES YOU EVERYONE LEFT YOU THEY'RE ALL OUT WITHOUT YOU HAVIN' FUN EVERYONE LEFT YOU NOBODY LIKES YOU THEY'RE ALL OUT WITHOUT YOU, HAVIN' FUN WHERE'D YOU GO?

DEAR J.

I got a ROCK and ROLL band
I got a ROCK and ROLL life
I got a ROCK and ROLL girlfriend
AND ANOTHER EX-WIFE
I got a ROCK AND ROLL house
I got a ROCK AND ROLL CAR

I play the shit out the DRUMS
AND I CAN play THE GUITAR
I GOT A KID IN NEW YORK
I GOT A KID IN THE BAY
I HAVEN'T DRANK OR SMOKED NOTHIN'
IN OVER 22 DAYS
SO GET OFF OF MY CASE
— Tunny

SAINT JIMMY
city

V. WE'RE COMING HOME AGAIN

HERE THEY COME MARCHING DOWN THE STREET
LIKE A DESPERATION MURMUR OF A HEART BEAT
COMING BACK FROM THE EDGE OF TOWN
UNDERNEATH THEIR FEET, THE TIME HAS COME
AND IT'S GOING NOWHERE
NOBODY EVER SAID THAT LIFE WAS FAIR NOW
GO-CARTS AND GUNS ARE TREASURES THEY WILL BEAR
IN THE SUMMER HEAT
THE WORLD IS SPINNING AROUND AND AROUND
OUT OF CONTROL AGAIN
FROM THE 7-11 TO THE FEAR OF BREAKING DOWN
SO SEND MY LOVE A LETTERBOMB
AND VISIT ME IN HELL
WE'RE THE ONES GOING HOME
WE'RE COMING HOME AGAIN

I STARTED FUCKIN' RUNNING
JUST AS SOON AS MY FEET TOUCH GROUND
WE'RE BACK IN THE BARRIO
BUT TO YOU AND ME, THAT'S JINGLETOWN
HOME.
WE'RE COMING HOME AGAIN   HAVIN' FUN!
NOBODY LIKES YOU - EVERYONE LEFT YOU - THEY'RE ALL OUT WITHOUT YOU

THOUGHT I RAN INTO YOU DOWN ON THE STREET
THEN IT TURNED OUT TO ONLY BE A DREAM

I MADE A POINT TO BURN ALL OF THE PHOTOGRAPHS
SHE WENT AWAY AND THEN I TOOK A DIFFERENT PATH
I CAN REMEMBER THE FACE, BUT I CAN'T RECALL THE NAME
NOW I WONDER HOW ~~WHATSERNAME~~ HAS BEEN
SEEMS THAT SHE DISAPPEARED WITHOUT A TRACE
DID SHE MARRY OLD WHAT'S HIS FACE
I MADE A POINT TO BURN ALL OF THE PHOTOGRAPHS
SHE WENT AWAY AND THEN I TOOK A DIFFERENT PATH
I REMEMBER THE FACE, BUT I CAN'T RECALL THE NAME
NOW I WONDER HOW ~~WHAT'SERNAME~~ HAS BEEN
REMEMBER, WHATEVER
IT SEEMS LIKE FOREVER AGO

WHATSERNAME 13.

REMEMBER, WHATEVER
IT SEEMS LIKE FOREVER AGO
THE REGRETS ARE USELESS, IN MY MIND
~~XXXXXXXX~~ SHE'S IN MY HEAD
I MUST CONFESS, THE REGRETS ARE USELESS
~~XXXXXXXX~~ SHE'S IN MY HEAD
FROM SO LONG AGO AND IN THE DARKEST NIGHT
IF MY MEMORY SERVES ME RIGHT
I'LL NEVER TURN BACK TIME

FORGETTING YOU, BUT NOT THE TIME

STARRING

BILLIE JOE ARMSTRONG
Guitar, Lead Vocals

MIKE DIRNT
Bass, Vocals

TRE COOL
Drums, Vocals

AMERICAN IDIOT

Words by BILLIE JOE
Music by GREEN DAY

Verses 1 & 2:

1. Don't want to be an A- mer - i - can id - i - ot.
2. Well, may - be I am the f** - got A - mer - i - ca.

Don't want a na - tion un - der___ the new me - di - a.
I'm not a part of a red - neck a - gen - da.

American Idiot - 6 - 1
PFM0506

all a-cross the a - li - en - a - tion,_____ where ev - 'ry-thing is - n't meant_

___ to be o - kay._____

Tel - e - vi - sion dreams_ of to - mor - row, we're not the ones_

___ who're meant to fol - low,_____ for that's e - nough_ to ar - gue.

To Coda ⊕

16

3. Don't want to be an A - mer - i - can id - i - ot,

...end solo)

Verse 3:

American Idiot - 6 - 5
PFM0506

JESUS OF SUBURBIA

Words by BILLIE JOE
Music by GREEN DAY

20

II. City of the Damned (1:51)
Moderately slow ♩ = 76

Verse:

center of the earth in the park-ing lot___ of the Sev-en E-lev-en where_ I was taught_
read the graf-fi-ti in the bath-room stall_ like the Ho-ly Scrip-tures of the shop-ping mall._

the mot-to was_ just a lie._____ It says,_
And so it seemed_ to con-fess._____ It

22

IV. Dearly Beloved (5:25)
Moderately fast ♩ = 154 (♫ = ♩³♪)
Verse:

30

V. Tales of Another Broken Home (6:31)
Moderately slow ♩ = 96

Verse:

live and not to breathe is to
lost my faith to breathe this, this
3. (Gtr. solo ad lib....

32

34

HOLIDAY

Words by BILLIE JOE
Music by GREEN DAY

38

Holiday - 8 - 5
PFM0506

40

The rep - re - sen - ta - tive   from Cal - i - for - nia has the floor.

Bridge:

Zieg   Heil   to the   Pres - i - dent gas - man,   bombs a - way   is your   pun - ish - ment.

Pul - ver - ize   the   Eif - fel Tow - ers,   who crit - i - cize your   gov - ern - ment.

Bang,   bang goes the   bro - ken glass and   kill all the fags that   don't a - gree.

42

rest of our lives.____

This is our lives____ on hol - i - day.____

*Sustained chord segues to "Boulevard Of Broken Dreams."

Holiday - 8 - 8
PFM0506

BOULEVARD OF BROKEN DREAMS

Words by BILLIE JOE
Music by GREEN DAY

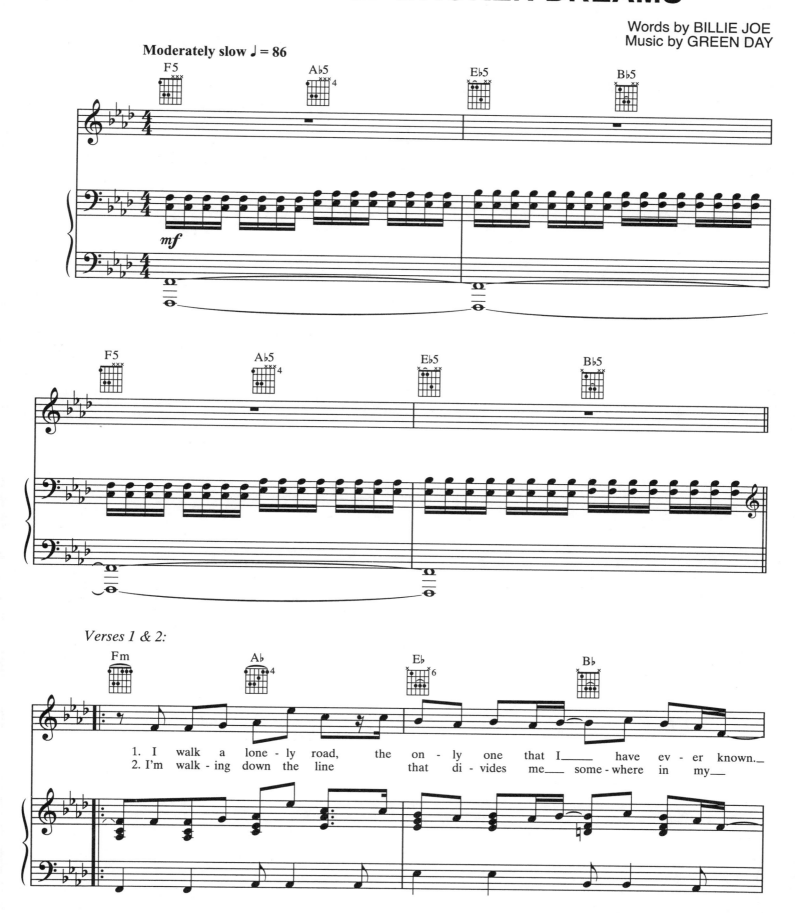

Verses 1 & 2:

1. I walk a lone-ly road, the on-ly one that I___ have ev-er known.___
2. I'm walk-ing down the line that di-vides me___ some-where in my___

44

Verse 3:

3. I walk this emp - ty street on the bou - le - vard__ of bro - ken dreams,__

48

D.S. ℅ al Coda

where the cit - y sleeps and I'm the on - ly one___ and I walk a...

Coda

___ a - lone._____

Boulevard of Broken Dreams - 6 - 6
PFM0506

ARE WE THE WAITING

Words by BILLIE JOE
Music by GREEN DAY

Chorus:

52

*Segue to "St. Jimmy"

ST. JIMMY

Words by BILLIE JOE
Music by GREEN DAY

Pre-chorus:

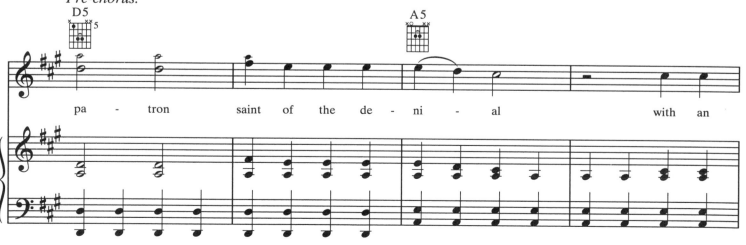

56

an - gel face and a taste for sui - cid - al.

taste for sui - cid - al.

St. Jimmy - 9 - 4
PFM0506

58

Saint Jim - my!

60

GIVE ME NOVACAINE

Words by BILLIE JOE
Music by GREEN DAY

Moderately slow ♩ = 78

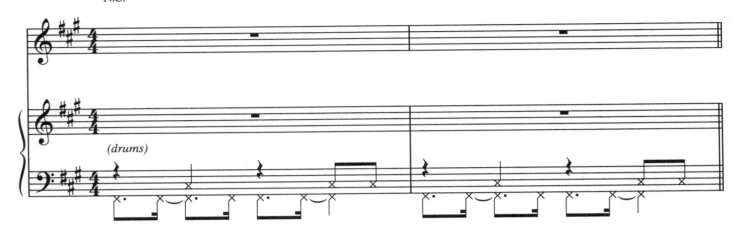

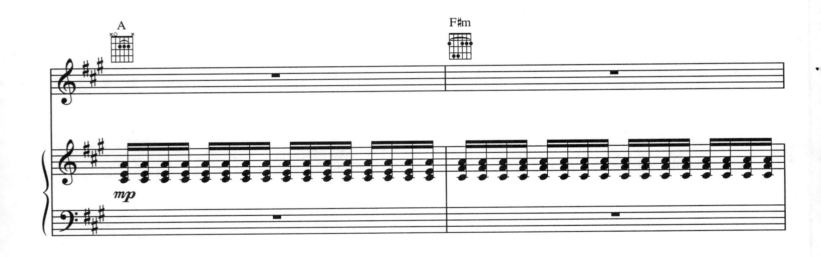

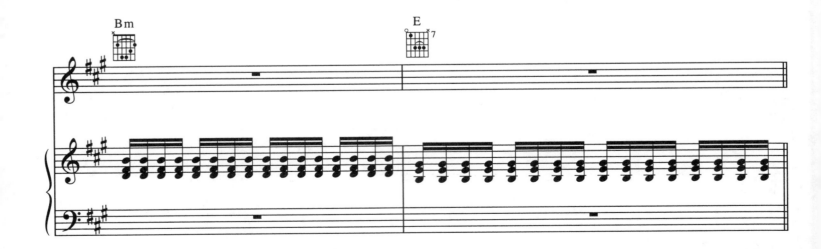

Verse:

1. Take a - way the sen - sa - tion__ in - side,_____
2. Out of bod - y and_____ out__ of mind,_____

bit - ter - sweet_____ mi - graine in_____ my head.__
kiss the de - mons out_____ of_____ my dreams._

It's
I

like a throb - bing tooth - ache of____ the mind._____
get the fun - ny feel - ing and that's al - right._____

I can't take__ this feel - ing an - y - more._
Jim - my says__ it's bet - ter than_____ air.__

I'll tell__ you why. }

so give me no-va-caine.___

Ah, no - va-caine.

66

Chorus:

Drain the pres - sure_ from_ the swell - ing.

This sen - sa - tion's o - ver - whelm - ing.

SHE'S A REBEL

Words by BILLIE JOE
Music by GREEN DAY

70

72

EXTRAORDINARY GIRL

Words by BILLIE JOE
Music by GREEN DAY

1. She's		an ex - traor - di - nar - y		girl___
2. She		sees the mir - ror of___ her - self,___
3. (Inst. solo....

Extraordinary Girl - 5 - 1
PFM0506

74

74

74
Extraordinary Girl - 5 - 2
PFM0506

LETTERBOMB

Words by BILLIE JOE
Music by GREEN DAY

Freely

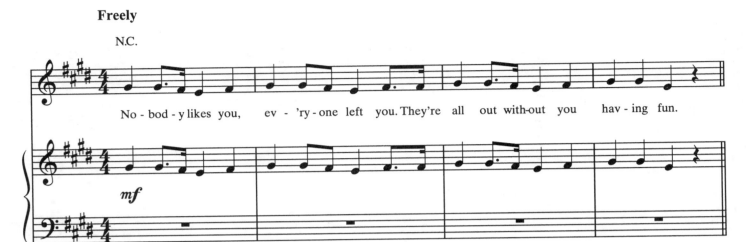

No - bod - y likes you, ev - 'ry - one left you. They're all out with-out you hav - ing fun.

Moderately fast ♩ = 164

1. Where_____ have all_____ the bas - tards gone?__
2. Where_____ have all_____ the ri - ots gone?__

Chords: F#5, A5, E, G#5, C#m, G#5, C#m, A5, F#5, B5, A5, B5

The un - der - bel - ly stacks___ up ten___ high.___
As the cit - y's mot - to gets pul - ver - ized.

The dum - my failed___ the crash___
"What's in love___ is crash now___

_____ in test,___ now col - lect - ing un - em - ploy - ment___ checks,___ like a
___ in debt,"___ on your birth cer - tif - i - cate.___ So

1.

flunk - ie on - ly a - long___ for___ the ride.___
strike the f*** - ing match___ to light this fuse,___

𝄋 *Chorus:*

f*** - ing life.   It's not o - ver till___ you're un -

der - ground.___   It's not o'er__

___ be - fore__ it's too late.

This cit - y's burn - ing.   "It's not my bur -

84

D.S. % al Coda ⊕ *Coda*

Made me the id - i - ot A - mer - i - ca.

Well,

E7

G#5

she said "I can't take this place, I'm
she said, "I can't take this town, I'm

C#m

A5

1.

leav - ing it be - hind." ___
leav - ing you to - night." ___

Well,

2.

E5

(Play 3x)

WAKE ME UP WHEN SEPTEMBER ENDS

Words by BILLIE JOE
Music by GREEN DAY

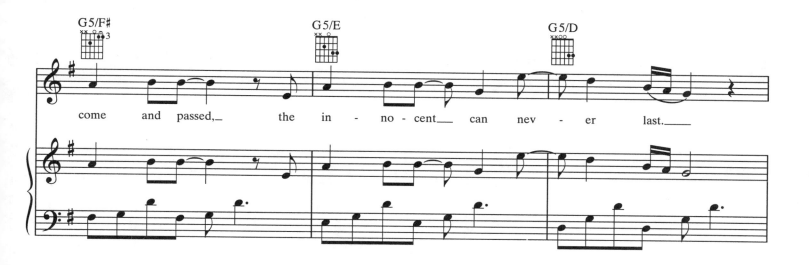

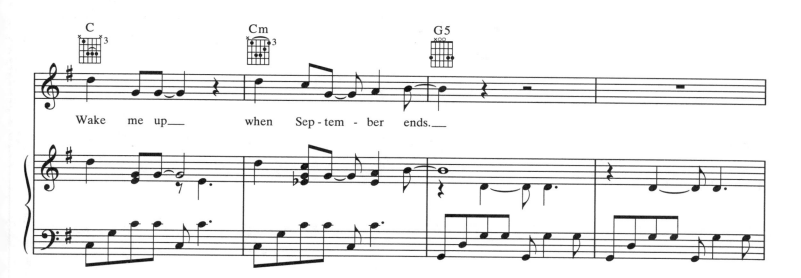

Wake Me Up When September Ends - 8 - 1
PFM0506

88

90

Verse 2:

2. Sum - mer_ has come and passed,_ the in - no - cent_ can nev - er last._

Wake me up_ when Sep - tem - ber ends._

Ring out_ the bells a - gain,_ like we did_ when spring_ be - gan._

Wake me up,_ when Sep - tem - ber ends._

91

Wake Me Up When September Ends - 8 - 5
PFM0506

92

Guitar Solo:

Verse 3:

HOMECOMING

Words by BILLIE JOE
Music by GREEN DAY

I. The Death of St. Jimmy (0:00)
Moderately ♩ = 112

1. My heart____ is beat-ing from____ me, I am stand-ing____ all a-lone.____

Please____ call____ me on-ly if you____ are____ com-ing home.____

96

II. East 12th St. (2:25)

Words by BILLIE JOE
Music by GREEN DAY

100

Chorus:

Verse:

102

Bridge:

Some - bod - y get me out of here.

An - y - bod - y get me out of here.

Some - bod - y get me out of here.

Homecoming - 21 - 8
PFM0506

III. Nobody Likes You (4:03)
Bright waltz ♩. = 76

Words by MIKE DIRNT
Music by GREEN DAY

Chorus:

1. No - bod - y likes you. Ev - 'ry - one
2. Ev - 'ry - one left you. No - bod - y
(Where'd you go?)

left you. They're all out with - out you hav -
likes you. They're all out with - out you hav -
(Where'd you go?)

Words by TRÉ COOL
Music by GREEN DAY

IV. Rock and Roll Girlfriend (5:20)
Moderately fast ♩ = 172

in' fun. fun. (Where'd you go, go, go, go?)
in'
(Where'd you

Jeez! *(sigh)*

Verse:

I got a rock and roll band,___   I got a rock and roll life.___

___ I got a rock and roll girl - friend,_

and an - oth - er ex - wife._____   I got a rock and roll house,_

I got a rock and roll car.___

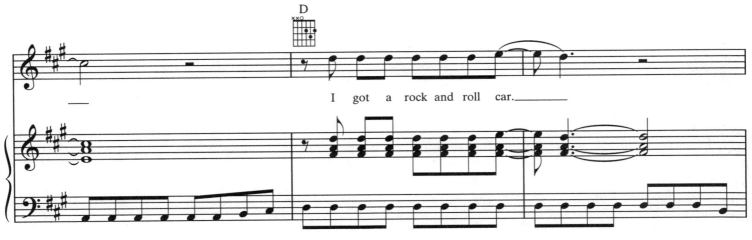

110

V. We're Coming Home Again (6:06)

Words by BILLIE JOE
Music by GREEN DAY

Homecoming - 21 - 16
PFM0506

114

WHATSERNAME

Words by BILLIE JOE
Music by GREEN DAY

All guitars in drop D: ⑥ = D

Moderately ♩ = 120

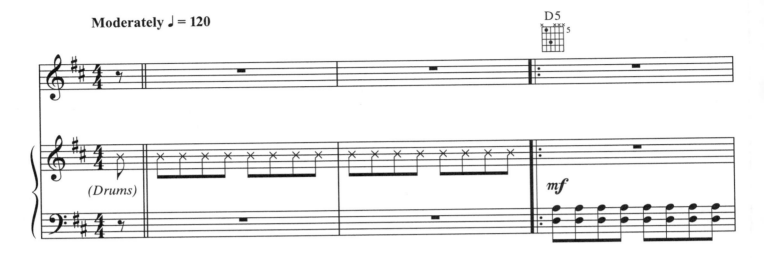

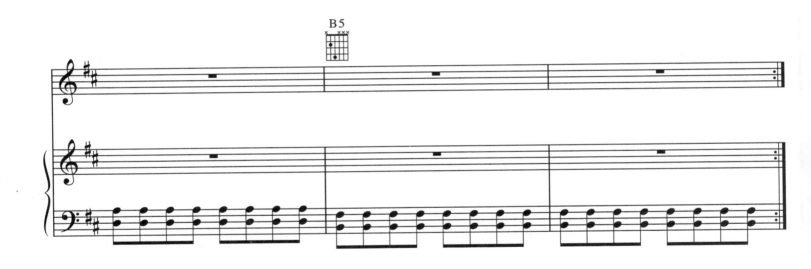

Verse:

1. Thought I ran in - to you___ down on the___ street.
2. Seems that she dis - ap - peared___ with - out a___ trace.

Whatsername - 7 - 1
PFM0506

118

Whatsername - 7 - 3
PFM0506

er - name__ has been.__